Westminster Hall
Medieval Ki

VISITORS to the Palace of Westminster are treated to a rich pageant of British history. Life-size stone statues of kings and queens from medieval times onwards stand out proudly amidst the profusion of vigorous, finely-detailed Gothic Revival carving which repeats in endless modulation over the impressive façades of Sir Charles Barry's winning design for the building. The richness of the Clocktower, the Victoria Tower and the other well-known exteriors is but a prelude, however, to the gilded majesty of the grand interiors in what is arguably the most important building of Victorian Britain. Cycles of impressive mural paintings decorate large areas of the walls, bringing to life important events throughout the nation's history. Carved reliefs and statuary embellish the grand interiors, and every surface including the tiled floor is extravagantly decorated with myriad patterns and colours.

The opportunity to design and construct a building of such impressive proportions and aspirations happened quite suddenly and unexpectedly on the night of 16 October 1834, when fire destroyed the majority of buildings which formed the Old Palace of Westminster, lighting up the London sky and being witnessed for miles around.

The Old Palace of Westminster on fire, 16 October 1834. View from Abingdon Street. Coloured lithograph by William Heath.

The subject of this booklet, Westminster Hall and the statues of the kings, goes back through history to a building which was to be inspirational for the Victorian Palace of Westminster. Westminster Hall was one of the most ancient and most important parts of the medieval Palace of Westminster, which, on the night of the fire, was saved from destruction by a combination of tireless fire-fighting and very good fortune, when all around was destroyed. The strong sense of history which Westminster Hall radiated – in use since the late eleventh century as the most frequent meeting place of the King's Great Council and since 1178 as the principal home of the Courts of Justice – together with its pure Gothic architecture of the medieval period, were to guarantee its survival at this crucial time. It was repaired and the roof timbers reinforced and included as an important part of Sir Charles Barry's New Palace of Westminster, which was begun in the early 1840s and all but completed by the time of Barry's death in 1860.

The hall's architectural pedigree could not have been more impressive. Built between 1097 and 1099 for William Rufus, its massive proportions would have attracted immediate importance as one of the largest halls in Europe. Three hundred years later, however, in the last decade of the fourteenth century, the Norman hall was to be transformed radically by King Richard II into the magnificent Gothic building with which we are now familiar. The hammerbeam roof took invention and design of medieval carpentry to new heights, allowing the impressive dimensions of the hall to be seen unhindered by the rows of columns which would previously have supported its roof timbers.

The remodelled hall was also to provide an important backdrop for carved decoration and free-standing statuary on a grand scale. This booklet will focus on six statues of kings from a series of thirteen which Richard commissioned for the hall during the 1380s. The six statues, which were carved by the workshop of Thomas Canon and gilded and painted by Nicholas Tryer, were sited inside the hall on the south wall in 1388 and it is here that for the last six hundred years they have remained, becoming like Westminster Hall, great survivors from the medieval age.

Richard's remodelling programme for the hall provided a further twenty-three stone niches on the exterior of the north façade lining both sides of the doorway. Above these were four larger niches, two on each tower. Into the lower niches were placed in 1400 the seven statues remaining from Richard's commission for thirteen. Two of the larger niches above were filled with bigger statues, also executed by Thomas Canon for Richard II, and presumed to be images of Richard II and Edward the Confessor.

At the coronation of Ann Boleyn in 1533 the number of statues in the lower line of niches had increased to seventeen, of which four were statues of queens. The four niches above had a full complement of four large statues by this date. Although the kings are shown in Hollar's drawing of New Palace Yard of 1647, the second half of the seventeenth century saw a ramshackle collection of pubs and coffee houses gather at the front of the hall, hiding from view the lower niches and statues. This was a period of sad decline for the hall, with the stonework falling into dangerous disrepair. In 1807, when the pubs and coffee houses were finally removed, only eight statues were found in the niches behind and it is probable that several statues were lost or stolen during Thomas Gayfere's repair work to the masonry of the north façade which followed in 1819–22. The much-eroded statues of kings, which now stand on the window sills on

The north façade of Westminster Hall, *c*.1795. Oil on canvas, attributed to Thomas Sandby.

the east wall of Westminster Hall, are believed to survive from those originally on the north façade of the hall. Two of these were acquired from Bayons Manor in 1962.

By comparison with the statuary on the exterior of the hall, the six kings inside on the south wall have enjoyed a fortunate history and some areas of the original carving are still intact. Directly beneath these statues at the south end of the hall the Court of King's bench and Court of Chancery have met over the centuries to deliberate and pass sentence, sitting initially in simple wooden enclosures which in time were replaced by more substantial structures. These were removed temporarily for occasions requiring use of the whole hall, such as state trials and coronation banquets, and in engravings of these events the six kings were invariably shown bearing silent witness. The first close study of the kings came in drawings made in 1784 by John Carter, which give key evidence on the condition of each statue, together with its respective position on the wall. Traces of the original polychromy were still visible at that date, but have subsequently all but disappeared.

The statues, like the hall itself, survived the fire of 1834, the thickness of the walls protecting them from excessive heat. They were then removed temporarily in 1835–7, at the time of Sir Robert Smirke's refacing of the interior of the hall with Huddleston stone, and again in the early 1850s when the present full-height archway was cut in the wall by Sir Charles Barry to create access into his grand entrance to the new Palace of Westminster beyond. The two flights of stone stairs also date from this period.

Interior of Westminster Hall, looking south towards the courts of Chancery and King's Bench. Coloured aquatint by Bluck after A. C. Pugin and Rowlandson, 1809.

The Court of King's Bench in the southeast corner of Westminster Hall. Coloured aquatint by Bluck after A. C. Pugin and Rowlandson, 1808.

The 1940s saw a new threat to the hall and the statues as the bombing raids of the Second World War brought increasing destruction; in 1942 the six kings were removed to Mentmore in Buckinghamshire for safe keeping, together with other valuable works of art from the Palace of Westminster. It was at this time that they were treated with limewash before being returned in 1946.

In 1986 an inspection of the statues by English Heritage revealed that the surface of the carved stone had deteriorated so badly in places that it was in danger of falling away. The final section of this booklet documents the extensive research and analysis which have been carried out on the statues and details the programme of cleaning and consolidation by English Heritage and Taylor Pearce Restoration Ltd which was completed for the Parliamentary Works Directorate in December 1994. The findings have been significant: with the layers of limewash removed to show for the first time in fifty years the true delicacy of the medieval carving, the importance of these statues is once again open to reassessment. Traces of the original medieval polychromy also indicate the sumptuous colours which the statues brought to Westminster Hall in the late 1380s and which today we can only try to appreciate.

Westminster Hall stands as it always did as a tribute to Richard II's architectural and artistic patronage. Today Richard gazes in silence from a different angle at the twin towers of his hall with their empty niches. In a reinterpretation of Richard's own ideas, his statue is one of many kings and queens carved by the Thomas Bank Workshop in the 1850s to decorate Sir Charles Barry's range of buildings on the west side of New Palace Yard. As for the interior of the Victorian building, Richard can also bask in reflected glory, for the symbolism which he employed so extensively in the carved ornament of Westminster Hall was revived by Augustus W. N. Pugin in his designs for decorated floor tiles, stained glass windows and historic wallpapers which are used widely throughout the Palace of Westminster.

The Great Hall and the Kings

THE SOLID SIMPLICITY of the Norman architecture of William Rufus's Westminster Hall, constructed at the end of the eleventh century, would have appeared old-fashioned and gloomy, although still impressive in size, by the time Richard II came to the throne almost three centuries later on 16 July 1377, at the age of ten. For Richard this was part of the Palace where he could make his mark and what he went on to achieve between 1394 and 1399 was undoubtedly a high point in royal patronage.

Richard's remodelling programme for Westminster Hall in the hands of Master Henry Yevele and Master Hugh Herland was a radical transformation of the old Norman architecture. Although the thick stone walls were retained, they were heightened, re-faced and heavily buttressed by Yevele. The north façade was given new importance by the addition of impressive stone towers which flanked the centrally-placed doorway. The Romanesque windows which lined the walls were replaced with those in the Perpendicular Gothic style, punctuating the upper parts of the walls. At the north and south ends delicately traceried windows of a much larger

The Great Roof Richard II with his master carpenter Hugh Herland inspecting the work of construction on the roof of Westminster Hall in 1397. Oil on canvas by Frank Salisbury, 1924.

RIGHT Carved wooden angel bearing the royal arms. Detail from the roof timbers.

size were introduced, increasing greatly the amount of light filtering into the hall. The most significant change, however, was the replacement of the old Norman roof timbers and supporting structure with Hugh Herland's hammerbeam roof, a masterpiece of design by any standards and clear evidence of the consumate skill of medieval English carpentry. The clever construction of this roof, which spread the massive weight of the structure down through a succession of wooden arched braces and beams to the stone walls below, succeeded in spanning at high level the full interior space of the hall – 239.5 × 67.5 feet. When compared to the arrangement of either timber or stone columns which are thought to have supported the Norman roof, the new feeling for space in the hall which the hammerbeam roof gave must have seemed all the more dramatic. The complex interplay of the structural wooden elements, linked with an intricate web of repeating vertical lines of Gothic pierced tracery, gives the roof a sumptuous delicacy as the timbers appear to rise effortlessly to the apex.

Magnificent architecture apart, carved ornament and sculpture were to feature significantly in Richard's plans for Westminster Hall. Here was a golden opportunity for the king to provide clear visual evidence not only that this was *his* hall but that his authority to rule was absolute. His badge of authority is repeated again and again both on the exterior and the interior carved decoration of the hall.

The king's personal emblem, the white hart lodged, chained and ducally gorged, is used liberally in the carved stone decoration of Westminster Hall. White harts of impressive proportions appear as label-stops on either side of the large window high above the north door. This is one of the dominant motifs of the hall, used to great effect together with the royal crest and helmet of the Plantagenet kings as intricately carved elements of the string course decoration, which runs around each of the interior walls immediately below the line of windows.

Close inspection reveals the spark of individuality which each of these carvings displays; the naturalistic modelling of the white hart's body and the design of the foliage behind differ considerably in detail, as do the interpretation of the chapeau and lion on the royal crests and helmets. These same motifs repeat with refreshing variation along the string course design. Undertaken by two Gloucestershire masons, Swallow and Washbourne, at the rate of one shilling per foot, this vigorous carving stands in sharp contrast to the much flatter and rather uninspired string course carving of the south wall between the sculpture niches which probably dates from the early nineteenth century.

It is perhaps no surprise that Richard's personal emblem is also a feature of the massive stone corbels, which punctuate the string course line and provide the point of support from which the principals of the hammerbeam roof rise. In order to fit the awkward space on the sides of the Marrestone corbels, the necks of the white harts are twisted round in a decorative if not entirely convincing way. Heraldic lions are squeezed into the opposite side angle of each corbel in similar fashion. Carved shields bearing the coats of arms of Edward the Confessor, five marlet birds set against a cross patonce and the royal arms of Richard II, decorate the front of each of these massive stone corbels in strict rotation around the hall. The royal arms also appear at a higher level on shields borne by angels at the end of each of the oak hammerbeams.

The main thrust of Richard's interest in carved decoration for the hall came in the form of over life-size, free-standing statues of kings, an idea which apparently predated his interest in remodelling the hall and had begun by 1384 with the commissioning from the Corfe marbler Thomas Canon of thirteen stone statues of kings. This was followed subsequently by a further two statues of a larger size. The Exchequer Accounts for 1384–8 record that Arnold Brocas, Clerk of the King's Works, received allowances for the expenses of the statues authorised by writ of privy seal dated 4 July 1388. Thomas Canon was paid £30 6s 8d for the making of thirteen statues, Walter Walton £28 for six stone niches and Nicholas Tryer £8 13s 4d for painting six of the statues in the hall.

It is unclear how Richard had intended this series of thirteen kings to be displayed within the Norman hall. Perhaps he was seeking to emulate Phillippe le Bel's Grand Salle in the Palais de La Cité in Paris, where an impressively long series of kings and queens were attached at high level to the columns and side walls of the hall; perhaps he intended the kings to be positioned between the Romanesque windows or indeed grouped on the south wall. In any event there seems to have been a change of plan by the time the kings were completed in 1388, for only six of the original thirteen were placed in the hall in Walton's decorative stone niches on the south wall. The two larger statues were placed on the exterior over the doorway on the north wall whilst the other seven remained in store until 1400 when they were placed in the line of niches after the remodelling of the north wall was completed.

Looking at the damaged condition of the six kings from the south wall today, it is difficult to visualise how they would have looked in Richard's time. Perhaps the most significant change over the centuries has been their total loss of colour. And yet gilding and vibrant colour would have been perhaps the most immediate and important aspects of the commission when they first stood in the hall. Visitors would have been impressed by these larger-than-life figures, each wearing a tall, deeply carved and brightly gilded crown and flowing emerald green and crimson robes. The large and carefully detailed brooches on the robes would have added to the sparkle of the statues, probably with pieces of brightly coloured glass set in the cavities. Against the contemporary context of images such as the Wilton Diptych and illuminated manuscripts, there is good reason to suspect that the kings' robes were richly patterned. Certainly the payment made to Nicholas Tryer of £8 13s 4d, almost two-thirds of the sum paid to Thomas Canon for carving the six statues, suggests not only the extensive use of gilding and expensive pigments (such as vermilion, which was imported from Spain), but also the time-consuming nature of the work. The number of paint layers applied bears witness to this slow process of 'finishing'. The rich emerald green for example was 'built up in various layers with the two pigments [lead white and verdigris] used in differing proportions to achieve the desired intensity of colour'. The pigments used in this commission, the gilding and the close attention to detail, are in keeping with other fine quality royal decorative schemes carried out towards the end of the fourteenth century.

Also of interest is that no subsequent repainting of the statues appears to have been carried out – certainly no indication of this was found in the paint analysis. Once in position on the south wall of Westminster Hall, the kings seem to have remained largely untouched. It must therefore follow that the areas of gilding and colour which John Carter recorded in his ink and watercolour drawings of June 1784 were indeed the remains of the original fourteenth-century polychromy. Sadly, those gilded and painted remains have long since disappeared.

The identity of each king has been a long-standing mystery and is open to debate. Although generally accepted that the commission for thirteen kings would have included all the kings between Edward the Confessor and Richard II, it is not clear which six kings would have been selected for siting inside the hall. Perhaps the original polychromy included a simple painted banner along the base of each statue, or perhaps painted heraldry on the kings' robes held the key. The question remains unresolved. The facial features of each king are of little help in the process of identification. Unlike Richard's tomb effigy in Westminster Abbey which was commissioned to be a good likeness, Thomas Canon's kings present a more stylised approach to the faces, with little differentiation between the facial features and certainly no attempt at portraiture. Images of Richard's royal ancestors were readily available in the form of tomb effigies in Westminster Abbey – from the sensitively sculpted gilt bronze effigy of Henry III by William Torel of 1272 to John Orchard's rather austere representation of Richard's immediate predecessor, Edward III, who died in 1377. The Westminster Hall kings were conceived, however, as architectural statuary to be seen within the context of the hall and not scrutinised at close range. The attributes of kingship and regal accoutrements were therefore of more importance than individual portraits. Likewise the crowns, robes and jewellery were not specific to any one monarch.

Regrettably, the original orbs, sceptres and swords which the kings bore have long since disappeared and been replaced with crudely executed plaster copies, which, like

TOP LEFT Detail of a white hart from the string course carving of the east wall of Westminster Hall.

TOP RIGHT The royal crest and helmet of the Plantagenet kings. Detail from the string course carving of the east wall.

Stone corbel bearing the coat of arms of Edward the Confessor. Detail from the east wall.

The six kings from the south wall of Westminster Hall, after cleaning and conservation completed in 1995.

the thick layers of limewash over the statues, serve only to weaken the impact which these statues must originally have made.

The recent programme of cleaning and conservation involved the scraping away of the layers of limewash and the quality of the original carving which has been revealed is unexpectedly fine. The idealised features of the kings, their thick locks of hair falling down in heavily stylised and deeply carved curls on either side of their heads, emerged from under the limewash. Fringes on the robes, previously completely hidden, suddenly appeared. The carving is vigorous, the detailing highly delicate and skilled, showing the hand of more than one sculptor at work. The statues have been executed with a full knowledge and understanding of French Gothic sculpture and bring to Westminster the prevailing fashion in carving. The gentle swaying postures of the kings, articulated through the deeply modelled folds of the drapery, are on the one hand decorative and on the other capture the move towards a growing naturalism. One statue in particular demonstrates this subtle shift in emphasis, the posture being less decorative and the facial features more individual and 'realistic'.

Richard was not to live to see his fine plans reach fruition. At the time of his deposition in 1399, although the bulk of the building work had been carried out, work on the twin towers of the north front was still underway. The hall was in this incomplete state when his successor, Henry IV, was declared king there on 28 September 1399. Henry continued what Richard had begun and the finishing touches were made to the hall in 1401, by which time the seven remaining statues from Richard's thirteen had been placed in the niches on the towers of the north façade and a further four statues had been supplied by William Chaddere for his tall stone pinnacle surmounting the north gable.

After this concentrated activity and hefty expenditure, Westminster Hall was to enter a long period during which no substantial change was made to its fine architecture. The disruption caused by the building work over, the busy daily life of the hall was once again resumed: the law courts sat in their wooden enclosures against the south wall and the whole hall was used on occasion for important trials and increasingly extravagant coronation banquets. Through these centuries of history, the six kings on the south wall bore silent witness.

Although the fine fourteenth-century English Gothic architecture of Westminster Hall has survived, patched and repaired, into the present age, many of Richard's statues of kings were not so fortunate. Those lining the niches on the exterior of the north front have all but disappeared and today only five of these, in damaged and eroded condition, are to be found in the hall, standing in window bays on the east wall. Only the six kings on the south wall have survived the passage of time largely intact. Theirs has been a long story of close association with Westminster Hall; its survival has guaranteed their survival. As for the future, the recently completed cleaning and conservation of the kings, described in the next chapter, has played a timely role.

Conservation of the Kings

IN 1986, following a request to lend two of the six statues to the *Age of Chivalry* exhibition at the Royal Academy, the condition of the six kings was inspected by conservation specialists from English Heritage. Their initial findings raised immediate concern about the poor condition of the statues and the loan proposal was declined. Thick layers of limewash, up to 5 mm deep in places, coated each of the six kings and this had masked very effectively the underlying problem of advanced decay and deterioration of the stone surface.

The full extent of the damage and the complexity of the conservation problem only began to emerge after a comprehensive condition survey undertaken by English Heritage. Areas of carved stone had blistered, others had become friable and disaggregated and in the worst instances the surface of the stone was delaminating and breaking away. In addition, small test areas of limewash removal exposed medieval carving of undeniable and unexpected quality.

Initial thoughts of carrying out the necessary remedial treatment on site in Westminster Hall soon changed in favour of a much more complex programme of conservation which would involve the painstaking removal of the layers of limewash and impregnation of the stone surface with consolidant. The work was to take until Christmas 1994 to complete, with the early years set aside for a series of tests and analysis. Work on the first three kings was undertaken by the conservators at English Heritage's Stone Conservation Studio at Vauxhall who coordinated the wide-ranging research. The final stages of this work were completed by Taylor Pearce Restoration Services Ltd, who also undertook all the work on the second three statues. The technical data in this section of the booklet have been compiled from their reports and findings.

Following the decision to conserve the statues off-site, the first problem was to strengthen the stone surface sufficiently to enable the safe removal of the kings from their niches and to transport them to the Stone Conservation Studio. In early 1988 the three statues from the southwest corner received on-site localised consolidation treatment using Raccanello Acrylic Silane E55050 applied either by syringe or pipette to areas of friable and disaggregated stone. Loose and flaking areas were supported with acid-free tissue, adhered with Polyvinyl Alcohol, so as to minimise the loss of original surface material. In this still highly delicate, though stable, state the three statues were carefully eased from their niches, taken down and transported in wooden cases to the conservation studio. Detailed surveys followed in the search for the safest, most consistent and most effective method of treatment. Petrological analysis confirmed that the statues were carved from single blocks of Reigate stone, a calcareous sandstone, with crowns made of Totternhoe stone, a chalky limestone. One of the kings from the second batch proved to be the only exception, with both figure and crown carved from a single block of stone. Both Totternhoe and Reigate, being finely grained stone, would have been highly suitable for carving of this quality. Stone analysis by X-ray diffraction was also carried out in an attempt to identify the causes of damage. Locally-derived sulphur compounds from atmospheric pollution were found, but the main cause of deterioration appeared to relate to repeated wetting and

Detail of the head of one of the six kings before the limewash was removed.

RIGHT Detail of the same head after the removal of the limewash and following consolidation treatment completed in 1995.

drying cycles. The most violent of these was undoubtedly the fire of 1834 when the south wall of Westminster Hall immediately behind the statues would have been exposed to intense heat before being doused liberally with gallons of water.

The search for traces of original colour was the final area to be tested. From the small samples taken by the staff of the wall paintings section of English Heritage's Paintings Conservation Studio emerged a tantalising flavour of the richly-coloured decorative effect which these medieval statues would have originally had. Although only minute and fragmentary traces of colour are now visible to the naked eye, small areas of colour have survived in the deeply recessed areas, such as folds on robes and intricately carved areas of the hair and beards of the kings. Examination of samples from these areas in cross-section and dispersion forms indicated that each king was dressed in robes of bright crimson red and emerald green. The medieval pigments used appeared consistent for each of the statues examined and included vermilion, red lead, white lead, verdigris, copper resinate, yellow ochre and black, and gold leaf. Up to four layers of paint were recorded in places, indicating that a richly-coloured finish was achieved, the overlay of contrasting colours suggesting decorative patterns on the robes.

The results of the wide-ranging tests and analysis which had been carried out pointed to one course of action: removal of the limewash and consolidation of the stone surface. The thickly-applied layers of limewash were compounding the problem of delamination of the surface of the stone and were an added complication to any

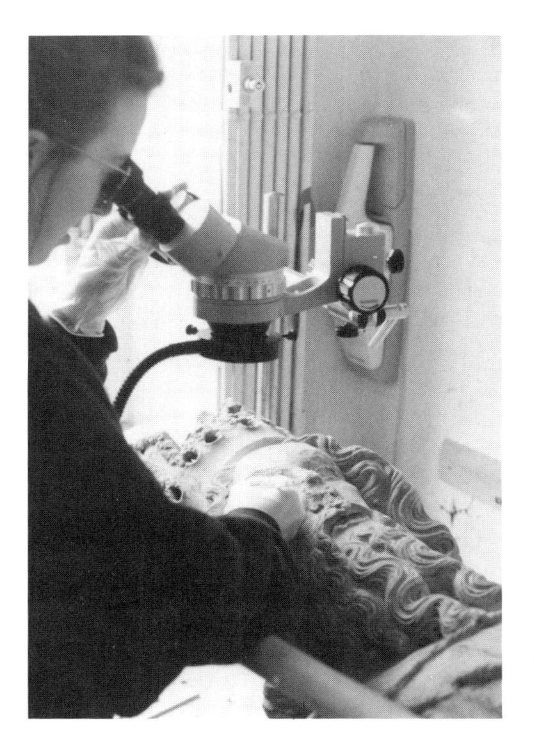

A conservator from Taylor Pearce Restoration Services removing limewash. Photo courtesy of Taylor Pearce.

Fire-fighting in Westminster Hall on the night of 16 October 1834. Watercolour drawing by G. B. Campion.

permanent consolidation treatment. They were also obscuring much of the finely-carved detail of the original carved ornament. Removal was the only answer and proved to be the most lengthy and painstaking part of the conservation programme. Looking through a binocular microscope at fifteen times magnification, the conservator could remove only a little limewash each day using a combination of scalpels, glass fibre brushes and dental instruments. The results were, however, impressive and prepared the way for the final part of the treatment.

In view of the extent and depth of the stone deterioration, up to 20 mm in some places, a programme of full impregnation of the stone surface was begun using a deeply penetrating synthetic consolidant to restore cohesion of the friable areas to the sound core material. Wacker OH, a silicon ester, proved the most satisfactory product and was applied in liquid form by hand spray or pipette. It gave strength back to the stone by re-introducing silica into the pore structure of the stone up to a depth of 80 mm.

The condition of the six statues, returned to their rightful place on the south wall of Westminster Hall, will continue to be monitored in the future. As for the kings themselves, a decade of careful analysis and painstaking conservation work has not only halted the deterioration of the stone, but by the careful removal of the limewash layers has served to raise the profile of these truly fine examples of late fourteenth-century medieval carving. Like the hall to which they belong, these statues are a glowing testament to Richard II's artistic patronage.

Portrait of Richard II, *c.*1394, commissioned for Westminster Abbey. Oil on panel by an unknown artist. Reproduced by kind permission of the Dean and Chapter of Westminster.

Chronology

1367 Richard born, son of Edward, the 'Black Prince' and Joan of Kent

1376 Death of the Black Prince

1377 Death of Edward III, Richard's grandfather. Richard ascends the throne as Richard II

1381 The Peasants' Revolt. The uprising, led by Wat Tyler, is put down by the young king

1385 Thomas Canon, marbler, carves thirteen statues of kings for the interior of Westminster Hall. Six are set up in niches on the south end-wall

1389 Richard formally declares himself of age and assumes full control of government

1390 Richard distributes badge of the white hart

1393 Remodelling of Westminster Hall begins, under the master mason Henry Yevele

1395 Richard impales the royal arms of England with those of Edward the Confessor

1396–7 The master carpenter Hugh Herland's hammerbeam roof erected in Westminster Hall

1398 Reconstruction of façade of Westminster Hall underway

1399 Richard deposed. Henry IV declared king in Westminster Hall

1400 Richard murdered

1401 Final touches made to the exterior of Westminster Hall

Acknowledgements

I am deeply indebted to Neil Stratford, FSA, Keeper of Medieval and Later Antiquities at the British Museum, whose enthusiasm about Westminster Hall and the statues of the medieval kings led to this booklet being written and the six kings being exhibited at the British Museum in October 1995. I am grateful also to all those at British Museum Press who have worked to make this small publication so professional.

I would like to thank the following colleagues from English Heritage for their advice and help throughout the conservation programme – Bill Martin and the staff of the Stone Restoration Studio at Vauxhall; Caroline Babington and Sophie Stewart of the Regents Park Conservation Studio; and Keith Taylor and his staff at Taylor Pearce Restoration Services Ltd.

George Garbutt's photographic skills, so important in recording the many collections at the Palace of Westminster, have generated all of the photographs in this booklet apart from those credited separately.

The works of art illustrated in the booklet are taken from the Permanent Collection of the Palace of Westminster unless credited otherwise and have been reproduced by kind permission of the Advisory Panel on Works of Art in the House of Lords and the Advisory Committee on Works of Art in the House of Commons.

First published in 1995 by British Museum Press.
A division of The British Museum Company Ltd, 46 Bloomsbury Street, London WC1B 3QQ

A catalogue record for this book is available from the British Library

ISBN 0 7141 0581 3

Designed by Roger Davies

Typeset in Palatino by Rowland Phototypesetting Ltd and Printed by St Edmundsbury Press Ltd, both of Bury St Edmunds, Suffolk

Front cover The north façade of Westminster Hall (restored in the nineteenth century)

Inside front cover The interior of Westminster Hall, photo © Woodmansterne